AF223560

ACCOUNTABILITY
IN THE
WORKPLACE:

Why Does it Matter?

DR. ANGELICA PIGMAN

Copyright © 2019 BY Dr. Angelica Pigman

All rights reserved. This book or any portion thereof may not be reproduced or used in any manner whatsoever without the express written permission of the publisher except for the use of brief quotations in a book review.

Printed in the United States of America

ISBN 978-1-7337907-6-5

Publisher: The Master Communicator's Writing Services

Contact: sharon@mcwritingservices.com

Dedication

This book is dedicated to my mother.

Table of Contents

#accountability matters

"At the end of the day we are accountable to ourselves - our success is a result of what we do."

— Catherine Pulsifer (Author)

"When people become involved in their government, the government becomes more accountable and our society is stronger, more compassionate, and better prepared for the challenges of the future."

— Arnold Schwarzenegger (Former Governor of California)

"My philosophy is that not only are you responsible for your life but doing the best at this moment puts you in the best place for the next moment."

— Oprah Winfrey (American Business Executive and Super Woman)

Foreword

"The greatest discovery of our generation is that human beings can alter their lives by altering their <u>attitudes of mind</u>. As you think, so shall you be." William James (1842 – 1910)

If there are any ingredients required for sustainable growth while exceeding expectations in any organization…it will be "accountability."

This is the much needed, but often overlooked, central plinth that stabilizes the spinning wheel and creates reliable and steady motion towards the right direction for organizational longevity.

However, many organizations and, or leaders has often been blindsided on the uniquely positioned benefit inherent in advocating and creating a culture of accountability in their organizations or workplaces.

Uniquely, and without a doubt, organizational effectiveness and its byproducts are determined by how much the human operators are willing, able, and ready to assume responsibility for and accept the outcome of their intuitive initiatives.

More and more managerial challenges require leaders to be accountable—to take initiatives on without having full authority for the process or the outcomes. Accountability goes beyond responsibility. Whereas responsibility is generally delegated by the boss, the organization, or by virtue of position, accountability is having an intrinsic sense of ownership of the task and the willingness to face the consequences that come with success or failure.

Through this guidebook you will learn how your organization and its leaders can create a culture that fosters accountability by focusing on: motivation, communication, building trust, while achieving a steady and desired performance.

The strength and wisdom in this book; "accountability matters in the workplace" further provides countless solutions and mitigating gateways for not only innumerable imperiled organizations from all strata of secular society, but also from the Whitehouse cascading down to every local municipality, and from start-ups to fortune 500s. Accountability will strengthen and stabilize the very dangling zipline of any organization, and create a mammoth return or harvest for both the "employer and employee."

Dr. Pigman meticulously x-rayed and articulated, both the importance and benefit inherent in a corporate environment where accountability is enthroned, while providing managers with specific advice on how to solve a leadership challenge to advance the understanding, practice, development of leadership for a greater benefit. Her extensive experience as a successful consultant, life coach, provider, relationship building advocate and manager in one of the nation's biggest sectors—healthcare, has no doubt enriched this must-read book.

"The benefit of truly accountable leaders is that they are able to create effective structures where their staff know what is expected of them, and can improve the business for customers." Jane Storm

By leveraging the contents and context of this book, you can unleash the true potential of "accountability in the workplace" and move your organization to the next level. This book teaches you that you can win by using the effective and compelling organizational skills presented herein. I recommend this book to all entrepreneurs, business owners, managers, supervisors and employees. It's a must read for everyone in all spheres of life.

Godfrey Ukoh DBA, OCP

Acknowledgements

I'd like to say thank you to my husband David Pigman, my dad Julio McCall, and my mother-in-law Judy McDonald. They shared many valuable critiques with me when reading my early drafts and gave me excellent advice. Thank you so much.

I would also like to thank my publisher and editor, The Master Communicator. I am extremely grateful and indebted to her for sharing her thinking, valuable guidance and encouragement.

Most importantly, I want to thank God, because without God I wouldn't be able to do any of this.

Introduction

Why talk about accountability in the 21st Century? Because accountability matters…The matters movement began in 2013 as a hashtag to express the concern of a community of individuals who were addressing various injustices in our nation. In the business world, corporate injustices such as human rights violations and abuses stem from a lack of accountability. This book was written to promote building healthy accountability cultures in the workplace to alleviate the injustices that severely influence the business world.

We also believe accountability matters because employee performance sets the pace for a company's success in the marketplace. Accountability is also a major concern in the workplace because it affects the tangible outcomes of a business organization and it directly affects their bottom line. No or limited productivity, no profitability!

Accountability matters internally because it fosters respect, trust, and productivity in a company's business environment. It matters externally because it fosters customer satisfaction, builds brand loyalty, and establishes a company's industry foothold.

In this book, it is our goal to thoroughly address the issue by defining the problem, suggesting viable solutions and reestablishing the importance of its consideration when mapping out business strategies for mission success in the 21st Century.

My "why" for this book

As a part of my dissertation, I did an extensive study on employee retention. Some of the factors that contributed to a high turnover rate were job stress, heavy workloads, poor management practices, few opportunities for advancement, and a lack of intrinsic and extrinsic rewards. I asked myself, who was ultimately responsible for employee retention, the employee or management? Or was it the responsibility of both parties? This process ultimately led me to the million-dollar question: "Who should be held accountable for this workplace dilemma?"

The lack of accountability, responsibility and trust in the workplace were conspicuous factors that contributed to employee dissatisfaction. This prompted me to dig deeper into the quagmire called accountability. The following questions started swimming around in my head. What is at the heart of this workplace dilemma:

- a lack of responsibility assumed by employees,

- their lack of trust in upper management;

- our blame-centered society,

- an unforgiving corporate culture;

- the introduction of the millennial worker and their laissez-faire way of doing things;

- the miscommunication of company expectations or

- toxic work cultures that are performance-based with little guidance.

I soon realized that the list could be as long as this book.

In *Accountability in the Workplace: Why does it matter?*, I will address the importance of accountability in the modern workplace; the modern worker's best posture in an accountability driven workplace; the benefits of employee motivation and accountability and how it affects employee productivity and performance; how to build an accountability culture and last but not least, examine management's responsibility for accountability in the workplace. This solution-based book is based on my research on some of the finest experts in this area and twenty years of work experience in the health care industry.

Denis Waitley states, "There are two primary choices in life: to accept conditions as they exist, or accept the responsibility for changing them." Assisting small businesses in creating a culture of accountability that is healthy and scalable for the good of all its participants is my way of accepting the responsibility to change the modern-day workplace. Why? Because accountability matters!

CHAPTER ONE

Accountability

What is accountability?

Accountability is an internal obligation of a person or organization to perform a certain task or function and report to other people for their actions. Accountability is the principle by which employees and management of an institution or organization should act in accordance with the will and intent of a company to provide goods or services for the benefit of its clients, customers, community, and stakeholders. Specifically, accountability is the commitment of a person or entity to accept ownership for the outcome of a specific task and its consequences, whether it's successful or not.

Often the term accountability and responsibility are confused because of their similar nature, but there are distinct variables that separate the two words. Accountability is a choice while responsibility is delegated.

Henry Browning, in *Taking Ownership of Your Responsibility,* defines accountability for leaders as, "…the acknowledgement and assumption of responsibility for actions, products, decisions, and policies, including administration, governance, and implementation within the scope of the role or employment position encompassing the obligation to report, explain, and be answerable for resulting consequences." That's a mouthful, but, yes, accountability depends on "you." If you are a solopreneur or independent employee, in the words popularized by President Harry S. Truman, "The buck stops here [with you]."

Accountability is everyone's responsibility. The organizational structure of a company does not minimize the level of accountability for its employees. Each person in the company's chain of command is accountable, vertically and horizontally, to perform at their highest proficiency based on the skills, talents, experience and education that they bring to the position. You and/or your team possesses the key to turn on the internal switch that breeds a culture of accountability in your company.

Accountability starts with leaders securing a greater level of commitment from employees and establishing a workplace culture that fosters engagement, empowerment and accountability. That environment is not one where employees are shaking in their boots because they are in constant fear of making mistakes or losing their jobs if a pioneering idea doesn't work out.

On the other hand, it is also not a place where employees aren't held accountable for late work, lack of punctuality, or incomplete projects. In an environment where there is little or no accountability, you may see the 80/20 rule in effect. 80 percent of the people are doing just enough to get by, while 20 percent of the people are doing most of the work. A lack of accountability is an indication that you have a very sick company.

Accountability is a primary contributor to the health and wealth of your company. The U.S. Office of

Personnel Management states that "it leads to heightened capability, increased dedication to the role, boosted morale, and higher levels of workplace satisfaction." Accountability also fosters innovation as staff members become more interested in the company going forward." The good news is that if your company finds itself on the opposite end of the spectrum, it's not too late to take the necessary steps to build a healthy accountability culture.

In the next section, we will take a closer look at how accountability works in the 21st century workplace.

How does it work?

In a perfect world, accountability has been one of the priorities in setting company goals and objectives. Not only are these goals strategically mastered for profitability and workplace harmony, but everyone from the janitor to the chairmen of the board is aware of what they are and how they contribute to building a culture of accountability. According to Browning in *Taking Ownership of Your Responsibility*, the leadership of an organization is responsible for setting the tone by implementing the five components of building accountability: support, freedom, information, resources, goal and role clarity.

Browning states that there are three types of support that are most crucial for fostering accountability. The first is an organizational level of support; the second centers around the role of the supervisor or boss; and the third is the human resources assigned to the task—the manager's team.[1]

Organizational responsibility limits the amount of freedom an employee has to be innovative and creative. Freedom invokes a mental commitment and personal contract to the success of a project. It also builds personal accountability.

Browning also discusses the importance of information access. He lists three major sources:

---

[1] Accountability: Taking ownership of your responsibility, Browning

- customer-focused (user-friendly) information access,

- supplier or resource-focused information access,

- and organizational system focused information access.

Resources—capital, personnel, and time—are critical in an accountability culture. They are often limited, but manageable, especially in a workplace environment that fosters innovation. Managers should not have to fight bureaucracy red tape in acquisitioning what they need in order to get the job done.

Goal and role clarity, are key components in the accountability puzzle. Management, cross functional teams, and employees need clarity on who and what they are accountable to; what outcomes they are responsible for; and in what areas they should submit or not submit to others.

We will go into greater detail in future chapters on how these elements foster an accountability culture.

The Difference Between Accountability and Responsibility

In this section, we will address the difference between a healthy accountability culture and a sick accountability culture. Imagine buying a house and not examining its foundation. Most homes have to pass a city inspection before they are sold and if there are cracks in the foundation, that spells out BIG trouble. Likewise, cracks or fractures in a company's accountability foundation can be devastating to all its stakeholders. Whether this happens in the boardroom, at the management level, or on the frontline within the workplace team, a lack of accountability can ultimately lead to the business's demise, unfulfilled employee potential and, at the least, missed business opportunities.

Companies with sick accountability cultures exhibit behaviors that undermine business results [cumbersome bureaucracy], cultivate fear and blame [victimization], encourage an entitlement attitude [the Lone Ranger Syndrome], and foster destructive collusions that undermine responsibility and authority [organizational silos]. As a result, the following symptoms may be evident:

- Poor employee performance

- Lack of trust

- Missed deadlines

- Questionable ethics

- Excessive cost overruns

- Chronic inefficiency

- Poor customer satisfaction

- Poor safety

- Low morale

- Inequity in rewards and promotions

- Lack of motivation

- Incompetency

- Lack of communication

- Miscommunication

- Lack of follow-through

Employees in this kind of culture are constantly fearful of negative repercussions or punishment for their performance or lack thereof. They usually believe that their efforts will not result in positive change. The employees literally avoid conflict and bringing attention to themselves because they are afraid that it just might be the spark that sets off their ultimate fears of being fired, downsized or laid off.

Why do organizations expect more of it?

Accountability plays a fundamental role in the commitment of the workers of any organization. It has a direct and significant impact on the profit and loss account. However, following the corporate scandals of Enron, WorldCom, and Tyco in the beginning of this century, interest in accountability has grown remarkably. The acute crisis of confidence that these scandals caused in the markets caused us to pay more attention to issues such as good corporate governance, information transparency, and conflicts of interest arising in relations with auditing companies. The Sarbanes-Oxley Act of 2002 was, without a doubt, a first step in the right direction: to increase accountability and good governance in listed companies.[2]

Accountability in the Age of Collaboration

In the Age of Collaboration, accountability has ceased to be an abstract concept. It has found its physical incarnation in all the new forms of expression and massive collaboration that today form Web 2.0. Beyond the countless ".com" newspapers, blogs, and wikis that daily comment on our social reality with total transparency, social networks have become transparent virtual countries, populated by hundreds of millions of inhabitants. This is the case with Facebook or Instagram. With their mobile phones, digital cameras,

---

email messages, and blog comments, these new countries have created a veritable wave of transparency of enormous utility. In spite of their detractors, these social networks are accelerating the changes our organizations need to meet the challenges of the Collaborative Era.[3]

We live in a world in which traumas and triumphs are instantly visible. In the words of Jonathan Schwartz, "Sunlight is not only a great disinfectant, it is a wonderful safety net because we cannot solve problems that we do not know or that are hidden from us." Similar to what has happened with the Internet and the markets—we have seen that the Internet has created more efficient markets. Accountability in organizations help to create internal and external networks that are more flexible and efficient. Although this is true, the resistance to accountability is still quite prevalent. The organizations we have built—both in the public and private spheres—are largely based on the opacity of

---

[3] Tapscott & Ticoll, 2003

their structures and their members' lack of awareness of the reality of the organization. Hence, the urgent need is innovating the management and moving towards more transparent organizations. To achieve this, we must design specific strategies that promote accountability.

In the book, *The Naked Corporation*, Don Tapscott and David Ticoll argue that in the Age of Mass Collaboration, companies have to accept the fact that partners, workers, customers, government, and the general public will have free access to all kinds of information about their organizations.[4] It is clear that people will have much more information than in the past and organizations must be prepared to take on this new situation by behaving and acting accordingly. Companies that try to limit access to information or ignore the forces of transparency are in danger of disappearing, unable to survive the new demands.

---

[4] Tapscott & Ticoll, 2003

Why?

In recent years, the business world has been characterized by technological advances and the integration of several national economies in the same market, generating a global economy. This innovative process that has characterized the world of business has been known as globalization. Globalization has meant a revolution that has made it possible to improve the economic indices of companies and their societies. It has also created challenges that will be overcome only by those companies that have evolved their strategic vision and have integrated their economic, social, and environmental dimension of the environment to which they belong, and become active players for contributing to sustainable development.[5]

Business leaders who have left the premise that their only obligation is to generate wealth and that their only interest are their clients, have adopted the strategy of ensuring *accountability.* They also contribute to

---

[5] Hoskisson, Eden, Lau & Wright, 2000

sustainable development in meeting the economic, social, and environmental needs of their main stakeholders or shareholders, which are part of their area of influence.[6] Communication of this added benefit to the public interest are key to building a business's accountability brand. The importance of this need to communicate and its importance in the business world is known as business accountability. It becomes a fundamental factor that contributes to the company's ability to develop and promote business ethics as a factor of competitiveness. The incorporation of transparency as a factor of competitiveness allows the company to manage its operations in a favorable environment that encourages investment and facilitates the generation of alliances with others who share their vision of sustainable development. This reinforces that transparency become a key factor for business development and society through accountability.

---

[6] Rubenstein, 2007

How can we contribute?

We can all contribute to making accountability a differential value in the organizations by making it a priority both on a personal and professional level. We can improve our success quota by utilizing the three basic components of cultural accountability in organizations.[7]

Active participation: Make accountability a part of the culture of your organization, a value practiced and applied at all levels. Accountability cannot succeed unless stakeholders know what they need to know and care about knowing it.

Relevant information: Accountability requires the provision of relevant information—whether positive or negative—to the interested parties in an open and transparent manner, within the legal limits and in a truthful, precise and balanced manner.

---

[7] Coghlan & Brannick, 2014

Responsible accountability: We must fulfill our commitments to accountability taking into account the interests of all affected parties, being sincere about the shortcomings and challenges, and ensuring the integrity of the company's operations.

Conclusion

Accountability is a force that companies can actively use to build and strengthen the trust of all stakeholders and to show their value in an increasingly global market. There are obstacles in our organizations that often hinder us from achieving full accountability. It is true that some of them are valid (as is the case of trade secrets or sensitive information about our customers). But numerous current business scenarios have shown that many of the financial services provided by entities that we thought were solvent were based on the opacity and lack of knowledge of customers regarding the real risks of the products offered (for example: Washington Mutual, Bernard L. Madoff Investment Securities, LLC, and Dynegy). In the short term, it may be possible to survive by maintaining a certain degree of opacity that makes our product or business model seem viable. In the long run, the truth ends up prevailing and customers can always find a better alternative.

The digital revolution and the Internet are crushing the way we do business at an accelerated speed, and changing the backdrop that has always hidden the reality of what happens in the back office. However, there are still only a few companies willing to accept and handle this new scrutiny. For most, accountability is an expensive and disturbing element that threatens their survival.

In this new environment, there is no use being in our "comfort zone" sitting quietly while acting as if nothing has changed in the last years. Accountability is a new force that is unleashing, at the moment, profound changes in all areas; changes that will definitely affect the future viability of all organizations. This revolution has uncovered a crucial aspect: the validity of our value proposition as a company is "just a click away." As never before, users now have all the information and can issue their verdict instantly with a single click. Blind trust and loyalty, as we have known them, no longer exist. Therefore, we have no choice but to reinforce and renew the value proposition of our company almost every moment of every day.

Accountability Matters: Case Study

Introduction

The impetus for *Accountability in the Workplace: Why Does it Matter?* was my dissertation study on the causes of high turnover in call centers. Building an accountability culture in any workplace starts from the top down, but the entire workforce must have a vested interest in improving the status quo in order for it to work.

At the end of each chapter, I will be sharing a snapshot, from the employee's perspective, of what contributed to the phenomena of high turnover in the call center I studied. Each case study will have a feedback, feedforward, and follow-up section.

Let's look at the definition of each of these words.

> *Feedback* — A process in which the effect or output of an action is "returned" (fed-back) to modify the next action. Feedback is essential to the working and survival of all regulatory mechanisms found throughout living and non-

living nature, and in man-made systems such as education system and economy. As a two-way flow, feedback is inherent to all interactions whether human-to-human, human-to-machine, or machine-to-machine. In an organizational context, feedback is the information sent to an entity (individual or a group) about its prior behavior so that the entity may adjust its current and future behavior to achieve the desired result.[8]

Feedforward — The reverse of a feedback. It is the "self-fulfilling prophesy" process that turns logical cause-effect relationships upside down. For example, if people believe the stock market is going to rise, their purchases drive up the stock prices thus creating the very situation they believed will happen. Similarly, if they think a bank is going to fail, their withdrawal of

---

[8]

http://www.businessdictionary.com/definition/feedback.html

deposits actually causes a healthy and strong bank to crash.[9]

Follow-up — Monitoring a job, enquiry, sale, etc., to get feedback on the schedule, requirements, effectiveness, or other such factors. Following up is a part of following through.[10]

Each of these processes are important when building an accountability culture that thrives in the 21st century marketplace. In the following case studies, feedback will be a direct quote from one of the employees in the call center. Feedforward will be the proposed solution for that feedback and follow-up will be a noted resource

---

[9]

http://www.businessdictionary.com/definition/feed-forward.html

[10]

http://www.businessdictionary.com/definition/follow-up.html

that specifically addresses the problem for further study.

We will look at such topics as how turnover impacts performance; employee perceptions of management's ability to perform their job; lack of adequate training and preparedness; and lack of motivation and morale.

It is my goal to make these case studies resources for you to help identify the possible cracks in your accountability foundation or help you implement preventive measures to avoid them.

CHAPTER TWO

Accountability for Employees

"Accountability breeds response-ability." — Stephen Covey

The enigma of who's accountable for performance in the workplace has been the key topic of multiple discussions in and around the proverbial water cooler. It just depends on who you are talking with. Management often points the finger at the frontline team which, in turn, points it right back. Meanwhile, there's an impasse in productivity and employee performance. So, what's the answer? Is employee accountability or the lack thereof responsible for the workplace quagmire? Well, let's take a closer look at what the experts say about "employee accountability."

Each employee should be aware that their contribution is important, valued, and necessary to the overall success of the company's goals and objectives. Simple enough but what does that look like from the top down? How is management defining the roles and responsibilities of their employees and how are they relating that expectation to them? Where does employee accountability start and where does management accountability begin? These are all legitimate questions that will be answered in this chapter.

In a business setting, accountability for an employee is often defined as honoring the degree of commitments employees make to the senior management and stakeholders as a whole. Accountability for an employee starts when they actually sit in front of the potential employer for an interview. In essence, the potential employee is saying, "I have the qualifications to excel in this position and I am willing to commit my skills, talents and intellectual resources to assist this company in achieving its purpose in the marketplace."

On the other hand, it is the hiring official's responsibility to make sure that the potential employee is the best fit for the position and will flourish in their businesses culture. In other words, the need for accountability in an organizational setting is a crucial management step towards attaining successful operations and attainment of overall business goals. Management has the ultimate responsibility when selecting personnel to hire employees that can and will perform to their highest level of competency for the good of the company. They also have the responsibility of providing a clear, precise, and substantial job description for the potential employee before and after they are hired. If the position requires additional training, it is assumed that the employer will provide it to adequately equip the new hire to perform the position. Management provides the appropriate resources, support, and guidance about employment and performance expectations.

It is also the responsibility of management to provide access to pertinent policies and procedures that affect all personnel (employee behavior and performance), career development goals, specific job stipulations, and organizational regulations that govern promotion and advancement. Once the employer does their part, the responsibility for accountability in the workplace shifts to the new employee.

Accountability starts with you

In *Accountability Leadership*, Gerald A. Kraines states, "Accountability is the obligation of an employee to deliver all elements of the value that he or she is being compensated for delivering, as well as the obligation to deliver on specific output commitments with no surprises." In simpler terms, employees are compensated to provide value through their optimal performance on the job when fulfilling their respective roles in the workplace environment. As a result, employees receive training, development, and benefits (professional and personal).

Kraines identified two types of employee accountability: fixed versus relative. He defines *fixed accountabilities* as those elements that obligate the employee to deliver outputs, use resources and processes exactly as detailed by the employer. *Relative accountabilities* are those that require the employee to utilize their intellectual capital and experience to make a judgement call in order to maximize value.

An employee brings their own feelings and beliefs about accountability to the workplace. These are intrinsic values that influence an employee's overall performance. An employer can create an atmosphere and expectation for accountability maximization in the workplace but the employee must possess a keen sense of personal accountability for it to work. In other words, *accountability starts with you*, the employee.

So, what is expected of an accountable employee in the workplace? In *Account-Ability: The Science of Human Performance*, Dr. Jim Sellner had this to say about what account-ability looks like in the workplace:

- Employees are set up and ready to go at the start of each day.

- People are engaged for 85% of the day.

- There is an absence of blame and a presence of self and shared responsibility for the good, the bad, the ugly, and the beautiful.

- Tasks and projects are done well, on time, and on budget.

- When projects are becoming off-time and off-budget, everyone is informed in plenty of time then adjustments are made to get back on track.

- People take responsibility for the specific duties that are part of their job.

- Team members hold each other to account.

- Employees work together toward common goals for the business.

In this scenario, employees and management both assume the appropriate levels of accountability and responsibility. From an employee perspective, accountability begins when they posture themselves to be engaged, empowered, and accountable. An engaged employee is one who is totally involved in the workplace and enthusiastic about their work assignment. They are eager to contribute to the overall success of the company. An empowered employee is confident when making decisions regarding their assigned tasks because they have the assurance of their management's support. An accountable employee will make decisions and, without fear of retribution, own the consequences of those decisions whether the results turn out to be positive or negative. When all the pieces of accountability are in place, the employees perform at their highest capability. Let's take a closer look at how employers can best equip employees to bring their "A" game to the workplace.

Delegation is not allowed

The Merriam-Webster dictionary defines the word delegation as, "the act of empowering to act for another."[11] Management delegates tasks, employment assignments, and projects to employees. Sometimes managers don't equip their employees to do the job. Every so often, delegation becomes "who gets the blame," "being called on the carpet," or "getting set up as the fall guy" in the midst of office politics. Managers may use the accountability card to get things done

---

[11] https://www.merriam-webster.com/dictionary/delegation

which they don't quite know how to do themselves. Every now and then, there are no established systems for implementing new policies or procedures. Also, the industry often does a twist or turn that is unexpected and management is trying to play catch-up, so the bulk of the responsibility falls on the front-line team. Sometimes, when you hear the word "accountability" it causes your blood pressure to rise.

According to Kraines, "Sometimes, this dubious ploy actually works." After all, when their boss says, "Just get it done!" many people can— through sheer willpower, brute force, and long hours—overcome managerial abdication, systemic dysfunctionality, and structural flaws. But the wear and tear burns people out and sub-optimizes the whole." Every company has accountability issues at some time in the life cycle of its business. Delegation or shifting the responsibility is the "easy way" out.

Here's a good place to define the difference between responsibility and accountability. Responsibility is task-oriented. It focuses on job descriptions and defined roles that are assigned by management. Responsibility for a task can be shared and can be designated before and after a job is assigned.

Accountability means that you are not only responsible, but you must answer for your actions to a higher authority after the job is done. The individual takes ownership of the task and ensures that it is achieved.

According to John G. Miller, noted authority on personal accountability, "Research has shown that when employees feel accountable for their work, they are more likely to contribute to solving problems and achieving organizational goals. Believing that if others would change, everything would be better—and then trying to force them to do so—drives people apart. The fastest way to enhance relationships is to remove the blame that breaks them down. Whether it's selling more products, building stronger connections or making political change, owning up and taking responsibility can help us move forward."[12]

Management can alleviate the delegation enigma by:

- Determining what, how, and when to delegate, as well as to whom based on in-house employee resources.

- Learning how to effectively and efficiently communicate the boundaries of a delegated assignment.

- Following up with employees and team members to ensure that they remain accountable for completing the task.

- Assigning the proper level of authority and responsibility to the appropriate personnel when delegating.

- Not completely relinquishing responsibility for the task to the assigned personnel. Monitoring,

---

[12] TIME, Hold yourself accountable—you'll be happier, BY JOHN G. MILLER NOV 19, 2016 1 MINUTE

managing, and motivating the employee/team to a successful completion.

- Identifying potential delegation pitfalls and developing a strategic plan to overcome them.

What employees can do

So, where does the employee fit in the accountability equation? Employees can hone their self-management skills in order to contribute to building accountability in their respective workplaces. David Weliver recommends the following in his blog, *Manage Yourself: 10 Ways to Make Yourself Accountable at Work, in Life, and with Money*:

1. Create a personal mission station — Define "why" you do what you do every day.

2. Set micro-goals — Mini goals that act as a springboard to a much larger goal.

3. Use lists wisely — Create a list to break down those larger tasks into doable, bite-sized pieces.

4. Make yourself accountable — Make yourself accountable for your time management.

5. Reward yourself — It makes you work harder to get something you want.

6. Do one task at a time — Contrary to popular belief, doing one task at a time and focusing on its completion gets you better results.

7. Emphasize your strengths, improve your weaknesses — Put your strengths on display and work hard to improve in your weaker areas.

8. Value your time — Maximize your productivity when you are working by focusing on the task at hand.

9. Seek feedback — Ask others how you are doing (co-workers, customers, management).

10. Review yourself — Perform a self-review consistently on a quarterly, semi-annually, or annually basis. [13]

The employee should also ask themselves the following questions when doing an accountability self-review:

1. Are you honest, no matter the consequences?

2. Can management depend on you to reliably deliver the desired results?

3. Do you take responsibility for your actions and refuse to assign blame to someone else?

4. Can you admit when you make a mistake and get the problem fixed to eliminate the possibility of the problem reoccurring?

If they answer "yes" to all of these questions, they are well on their way to mastering personal accountability. Yet, there is an interior work that takes place inside of each individual. First, the employee must see the

---

[13] https://www.moneyunder30.com/manage-yourself-10-ways-to-make-yourself-accountable-at-work-in-life-and-with-money

purpose behind their commitment and loyalty to the business. Acknowledging their value to the organization is a key management responsibility that goes beyond the yearly awards ceremony or the gold watch at retirement. It's a continuous process both internally (e.g. verbal affirmation from management and team members) and externally (e.g. customer satisfaction surveys).

Fostering a work environment that promotes employee autonomy is also key to creating an atmosphere of accountability. When one feels that they have a meaningful impact on the outcome of a project, mission, or job assignment, it builds personal accountability.

Effectively communicating expectations and being totally transparent allows everyone the privilege of knowing exactly where they fit in the accountability puzzle. It also builds trust and a strong working relationship.

In our current economic climate, employees are concerned about losing their jobs more than any other time in history. Jennie E. Brand had this to say about job security in *The Far-Reaching Impact of Job Loss and Unemployment*:

> "Widespread job insecurity, waves of job loss, and associated periods of unemployment and income loss have characterized the last several decades in the U.S. (Farber 2010; Farley 1996; Kalleberg 2000, 2009; Kletzer 1998; Wetzel 1995). Most Americans believe that employment stability has declined (Hollister 2011), and job displacement is now considered a common feature of the U.S. labor market. The macroeconomic trends commonly associated with worker displacement include: technological change; foreign trade and the shift to production offshore to take advantage of low-wage foreign workers; immigration; firms' greater use of outside suppliers, subcontractors, and partners, and the paring

down of the activities of the firm; the shift in U.S. consumption from manufactured goods to services; poor firm management; weakened labor unions; and regional and national economic downturn."[14]

Workers not wanting to lose their jobs has an adverse effect on building accountability. When this fear is nurtured, the workplace becomes highly toxic and rigidly competitive. In order to alleviate this undue stress on employees that prohibits them from speaking up, accepting new processes and policies, and embracing accountability, you must create a non-punitive environment of psychological safety.

Maslow's *Hierarchy of Needs* is a great place to start to get an understanding of what motivates people to achieve certain needs. He focused on what makes people happy and the things that they do to achieve

---

[14] The Far-Reaching Impact of Job Loss and Unemployment*Jennie E. Brand - https://www.ncbi.nlm.nih.gov/pmc/articles/PMC4553243/#S 1title

that goal. Maslow believed that these needs play a major role in motivating behavior. He defined physiological, security, social, and esteem needs as deficiency needs, which are influenced by lack. Satisfying these lower-level needs are important to employers because an unhappy worker equates to an unhappy workplace. The highest level of the pyramid is self-actualization, which is a growth need. This need stems from a person's desire to grow as an individual. (Maslow also stated that the order in which these needs are fulfilled does not always follow the standard progression of the pyramid.)

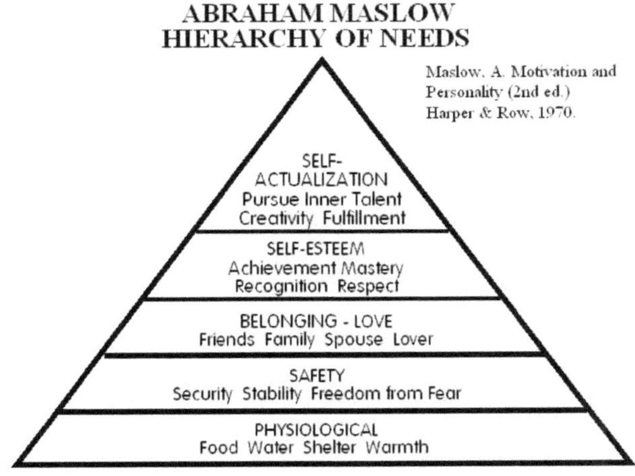

A person's need for stability and security can prohibit them from performing at their highest capability, if they fear losing their job. This also threatens their basic physiological need for food, water, and shelter. On the other hand, an environment that promotes autonomy, for example, may actually help an individual achieve their need for self-actualization.

Employees are an organization's most valuable resource. Businesses have the distinct honor of providing an employee with the opportunity to be more than just a warm body in an office cubicle. In the right environment, the employees can actually be what they dream to be, while vesting in the success of their company.

> "Encouraging employees to take responsibility for their decisions and actions, and to accept the associated outcomes, can result in extensive benefits for organizations. However, it is crucial that such circumstances take place in a

supportive environment." — Craig Dowden, Ph.D. in PeopleTalk

How to increase employee accountability in the workplace

The need for employee accountability is predicated on the organization's ability to understand their workforce, clearly communicate expectations, and promote employee growth.

In some workplace environments, managers are hesitant to address a lack of accountability because they abhor confrontation. If employee accountability is not addressed, it could send a demotivating and indirect message to the team. This could result in resentment and overall low performance from other team members.

That may mean having a difficult conversation with an employee without being confrontational. It also requires that management addresses the employee's poor performance as soon as possible while simultaneously considering the employee's feelings.

Often, bringing clarity to what's expected with SMART goals may alleviate confusion in the future. SMART stands for S—Specific, M—Measurable, A—Attainable, R-Relevant, and T—Timely. This method improves communication between the employee and their supervisor by being concise and providing measurable outcomes.

Follow through on anything you said you would do and follow up with the employee with a written transcript (email) about what was addressed, mutually agreed upon solutions, expectations and desired employee behavior in the future. Also, follow-up in person, the day after the conversation and periodically during the work week.

Remember to praise them when they are performing at the expected level and always relate your expectations in a positive manner.

Conclusion

There are a good number of reasons for organizations to adopt the notion of employee accountability. Trust is a pertinent aspect that is essential in most relationships in different workplace settings. Consequently, accountability improves employee performance. It eliminates the notion of time and effort spent on distracting actions and other unproductive behaviors. A work environment that fosters accountability promotes ownership. This is the case when personnel are made accountable for their actions. They are being shaped to always value their work and that of everyone on their team. Accountability enhances confidence among personnel. If done in the proper and correct manner, accountability is able to improve team member's skills and level of confidence. In fact, it is important that leaders should not mistake the notion of accountability as a form of controlling behavior, but as a means to engage, empower and hold employees accountable.

Accountability Matters Case Study One: Turnover and Employee Performance

Does Stress Influence Employee Performance?

Job stress is a major source of stress for employees in the workplace. Additional contributing factors such as having minimal control on the job and additional demands have increased the probability of a stressful workplace. Internal factors such as a lack of job security juggled with outside factors such as achieving a work-life balance can be overwhelming. According to The American Institute of Stress, "stress is a highly personalized phenomenon." [15] When faced with certain workplace scenarios, different people respond in different ways for different reasons. In this case study, we will take a look at the dissertation, *Employee Retention in an Organization Call Center,* to get a snapshot of the contributing factors to high turnover rates in this industry. You may see some familiar feedback from your organization.

Feedback — The job is stressful.

---

[15] https://www.stress.org/workplace-stress

Reference: Research Question One — "What working conditions contribute to call center CSRs leaving the call center?"

The frequently occurring theme for the question was that the job is stressful. This theme refers to the perception that the working conditions of the job being stressful contributes to call center CSRs leaving the call center. In the 14 interviews that were conducted, it was mentioned 33 times that the job is stressful.

For example, participant 18 said:

"[Employee turnover] definitely makes it more stressful. Under so much stress, it is a little bit harder to focus and get everything done because we have certain limits that we have to meet or exceed, and different quotas. It definitely affects the work environment in that way.

Later, the same respondent stated:

"Well, because of the stress that is created, a lot of the employees feel like they may not necessarily be getting the respect or benefits or anything that they, I guess, feel like they're entitled to. This kind of affects their thinking and how they act at work especially. It's really negative."

Feedforward

The general consensus among the employees queried identified stress on the job as a key contributor to the high turnover rate. First, the expectation in the call center industry is that businesses will have a high turnover rate due to the nature of the job. This expectation influences managerial decisions and often limits the investment that management makes in employees. This attitude is infectious and flows from the top down. In order to get a different result on the call center floor, management would have to be willing to change this paradigm by investing more in their employees in regards to training, team management, employee empowerment and building a more collaborative workplace.

Follow-up

For more information about stress in the workplace, check out the *NIOSH Stress…At Work* report by the U.S. Department of Health and Human Services.

Here are a few highlights from that report:

- 40% of workers reported their job was very or extremely stressful.

- 25% view their jobs as the number one stressor in their lives.

- 75% of employees believe that workers have more on-the-job stress than a generation ago.

- 29% of workers felt quite a bit or extremely stressed at work.

- 26% of workers said they were "often or very often burned out or stressed by their work.

- Job stress is more strongly associated with health complaints than financial or family problems.

Another good resource is John G. Miller's *QBD! The Question Behind the Question: Practicing Personal Accountability at Work and in Life*. QBD provides a practical method for building and implementing personal accountability by eliminating blame, and eradicating a victim-mentality, and procrastination.

CHAPTER THREE

Accountability and Motivation

"Appreciate everything your associates do for the business. Nothing else can quite substitute a few well-chosen, well-timed, sincere words of praise. They're absolutely free and worth a fortune." — Sam Walton

For the first time in history, there are currently five generations (The Silent Generation, Baby Boomers, Generation X, Generation Y—aka Millennials, and Generation Z) in the workplace. So, employee motivation can realistically depend on who you are talking to and what's important to them both inherently and externally. The one-size-fits-all method of motivation could render the opposite effect in an accountability challenged workplace. Let's set a baseline for what employee motivation looks like and then examine various proven strategies that foster it in today's workplace.

In *What Is the Definition of Employee Motivation?*, Ashley Donohoe states that, "Employee motivation describes how committed an employee is to his job, how engaged he feels with the company's goals and how empowered he feels in his daily work."[16] Some business leaders feel that a paycheck should be enough motivation for an employee to adequately perform their job responsibilities. Although it is a viable incentive, employees are human beings who require a bit more to go above and beyond the call of duty on any given day. The challenge for businesses is to create a work environment that is both intrinsically satisfying and extrinsically encouraging for all employees.

Do accountability and motivation work together?

So why do companies need motivated employees? They need them to do their jobs proficiently in order to accomplish the company's mission and fulfill their vision for growth. A winning team does more than win the game; they inspire others to do likewise and encourage them to exceed their perceived limitations. They also share new and innovative strategies for meeting difficult goals and objectives. Donohoe adds

---

[16] https://bizfluent.com/about-5387352-definition-employee-motivation.html

that, "Small businesses need motivated workers who strive to work effectively and efficiently. Motivated employees not only contribute positively to the company's overall mission and direction but also help reduce costs, bring creativity and solve challenging problems." Wow!

Some employers may understand that this is necessary but they don't know how to create a motivating environment because people have never been a priority. Yet, in this age, your business's success depends on your ability to master employee relations, communicate, relate to those issues that are important to the people who work for you and build a strong accountability culture.

Where does accountability fit into the picture when it comes to motivating employees? Accountability lays the groundwork for motivation. It's the "what" you are being motivated to accomplish. It's those clear and precise goals and objectives that you're aspiring to reach in order to fulfill the company's mission. Motivation fuels an employee's personal integrity, builds a cohesive team spirit, and strengthens the trust relationship between an employer and their employees. When implemented correctly, accountability improves employee morale. Simply speaking, businesses that create a culture of accountability recognize and reward hard work.

One of the staples when building a good accountability culture is having a management team that excels in employee motivation. David McClelland identified a theory that could help you motivate your employees based on their personality type.

McClelland's Human Motivation Theory

In an earlier chapter, we discussed Maslow's *Hierarchy of Needs* (1940's). Later, in 1961, David McClelland built on Maslow's work in his book, *The Achieving Society*. He identified three main motivators which he believed we all have: a need for achievement, a need for affiliation, and a need for power. People have different characteristics depending on their dominant motivator which is learned.

The Mind Tools Content team had this to say in an article titled, *McClelland's Human Motivation Theory: Discovering What Drives Members of Your Team.* McClelland's premise is "regardless of our gender, culture, or age, we all have three motivating drivers, and one of these will be our dominant motivating driver. This dominant motivator is largely dependent on our culture and life experiences.

Achievement

People motivated by achievement need challenging, but not impossible, projects. They thrive on overcoming difficult problems or situations, so make sure you keep them engaged this way. People motivated by achievement work very effectively either alone or with other high achievers.

When providing feedback, give achievers a fair and balanced appraisal. These people want to know what they're doing right—and wrong—so that they can improve.

Affiliation

People motivated by affiliation work best in a group environment. Whenever possible, try to integrate them into a team (versus having them work alone). They also don't like uncertainty and risk. Therefore, when assigning projects or tasks, save the risky ones for other people.

When providing feedback to these people, be personal. It's still important to give balanced feedback, but if you start your appraisal by emphasizing their good working relationship and your trust in them, they'll likely be more open to what you say. Remember that these people often don't want to stand out, so it might be best to praise them in private rather than in front of others.

Power

Those with a high need for power work best when they're in charge. Because they enjoy competition, they do well with goal-oriented projects or tasks. They may also be very effective in negotiations or in situations in which another party must be convinced of an idea or goal.

When providing feedback, be direct with these team members. And keep them motivated by helping them further their career goals." [17]

In order to effectively implement McClelland's theory, you must be acutely aware of your employees' strengths and weaknesses. You also need to possess the willingness to commit to building a better work environment where everyone wins. Below, you will find a practical list of motivators for your employees.

---

[17] https://www.mindtools.com/pages/article/human-motivation-theory.htm

- Be respectful and treat employees like adults

- Be reasonable and clear in your expectations

- Minimize the number of rules and policies in the work environment and make them memorable

- Be approachable

- Be communicative

- Demonstrate trust

- Provide instant employee recognition when feasible

- Give valuable feedback

- Provide coaching and mentoring from managers and leaders

- Provide employee benefits and perks

- Be transparent about issues that are important to employees

- Provide a decent compensation

- Be sensitive to employee needs by helping them achieve a healthy work/life balance

- Involve people in the decision-making process

- Encourage your employees to use accountability as motivation to achieve their professional and personal goals

Fran Fisher had this to say about true motivation, "Consider this: instead of trying to motivate someone with rewards, find what interests them and also call on their strengths. You will have a more energized and engaged employee who is more productive, responsible and accountable."[18]

Motivation in the workplace

Achieving a delicate balance between organizational goals and an individual employee's interests is not impossible. However, it requires that management be cognizant of the WIIFM (What's In It For Me)

---

[18] https://franfishercoach.com/motivation-and-accountability/

objectives of its employees. There's trouble in the workplace when the drive for organizational performance is misaligned with the personal needs and goals of the workforce. People need to understand how they will benefit from their investment in your organization beyond the weekly paycheck. Their buy-in to the company's performance expectations and its fairness dictates the level of their contribution. You can avoid confusion in the workplace by:

- Showing genuine interest in what is important to your workforce

- Supporting your employees in achieving their goals

- Reciprocating by sharing what your organization cares about

When you build a caring culture in the workplace, your employees will care about what you care about. One of my favorite quotes comes from John C. Maxwell, noted leadership expert and author. He said, "People never care how much you know until they know how much you care."

Productivity: how to improve it

Once you've established a workplace culture that fosters motivation, your next goal would be to establish a system that evaluates what works and what doesn't. One of the key metrics in making that determination is productivity. In an accountability culture, increased productivity is an expected outcome. To ensure that you have the proper check points in place to gauge your success, here are a few recommendations. Make sure that the workplace environment is at its optimum for employee performance by:

1. Giving your team members ownership; let them make their own decisions and empower them to be accountable for their work.

2. Setting communication expectations by making it a priority for the project manager to effectively communicate with their team.

3. Knowing the team members' strengths, weaknesses, and hidden talents so you allocate tasks accordingly.

4. Encouraging team camaraderie by occasionally incorporating team-building exercises and having some fun.

5. Utilizing a user-friendly project management software that brings everything and everyone together in one place.

6. Ensuring that the physical environment (lighting, furniture, resources, and equipment) and overall office temperament is conducive for peak productivity.

7. Utilizing appropriate incentives to motivate employees based on their desires.

8. Not micro-managing them.

9. Acknowledging employees when a job is well done.

10. Giving employees the vital feedback that they need to improve their performance and cultivate a culture of open dialogue.

Conclusion

Motivation and accountability are fraternal twin concepts that work better together and do poorly otherwise. According to the American Psychological Association's *2016 Work and Well-Being Survey*, workers are more motivated to work hard when they feel valued. [19] It's a win-win situation for any employer who is willing to invest their time in establishing an environment where accountability and motivation go hand in hand. Happy employees perform at their highest capacity because they know you care not only about the bottom line but also about them.

---

[19] https://www.apaexcellence.org/assets/general/2016-work-and-wellbeing-survey-results.pdf

Accountability Matters Case Study Two: Lack of Employee Motivation and Morale

Employee Motivation

Employee motivation and low productivity cannot be blamed on the employee entirely. The workplace environment, culture, and conditions have a great deal of influence on performance outcomes.

In this case study, we will take a look at the dissertation, *Employee Retention in an Organization Call Center,* and get a snapshot of the contributing factor to high turnover rates in this industry based on employee motivation. You may see some familiar feedback from your organization.

Feedback — Lack of motivation and morale.

Reference: Research Question Three — "What other environmental factors contribute to the CSRs leaving the call center?"

One of the frequently occurring themes for this question was the lack of motivation and morale. It refers to the CSRs' perception that there was a general lack of motivation and morale that contributed to the call center CSRs leaving the call center. The lack of motivation and morale was mentioned 20 times in 9 interviews.

For example, participant 15 said:

"Well, because of the stress that is created, a lot of the employees feel like they may not necessarily be getting the respect or the benefits or anything that they, I guess, feel like they're entitled to. This kind of affects their thinking, how they act at work especially. It is negative.

Motivation is just something that really just pushes you. You have to find that within yourself. You can't really depend on other people to help motivate you because a lot of times you won't get that, especially in the work environments where it is a lot of high turnovers. You're not going to get that from management. You're going to get more of almost the opposite. You don't want to. You do not feel like working because it is so much stress."

When asked how employee turnover affected job performance, participant 15 said, "My morale is below zero right now, minus something. (Laughs). I'm not like a zombie. There's no motivation to do anything. I'm just here. I'm like a zombie; I come to work and I leave. There's no push; there's no drive."

Feedforward

The general consensus of the employees queried identified that the lack of employee motivation and morale were largely influenced by the culture. This company would have to implement widespread changes in their setup to improve the productivity of its workforce. For example, if you hire the best call center representatives in the world and place them in a toxic work environment, you would get the same negative results.

It would also require a paradigm shift in the thinking of upper level management. Sometimes employees are like diamonds in the rough. Invest in them and they will often reciprocate. Show them that they are appreciated and valued and they may increase their productivity. Hiring the right kind of employee for the job and training them to be successful also helps build their confidence so that they are in a better position to reach their maximum potential.

Follow-up

For more information about employee motivation and morale, check out the _2018 Work and Well-Being Survey_ carried out by the American Psychological Association.

Here are a few highlights from that report:

"Chronic job stress, being overworked and feeling a lack of support to take time off—these are issues facing many U.S. workers. Too often, the burden falls on individual employees to make the best use of vacation time, recharge and return to the fray only to face the same larger systemic issues that wore them down in the first place. As this year's _Work and Well-Being Survey_ findings show, employees need the support of an organizational culture that allows them to recover from stress and function at their best on and off the job. The *Work and Well-Being Survey* provides a snapshot of the U.S. workforce, including employee well-being, attitudes and opinions related to workplace policies and practices. Among other things, this year's survey explores the effect of time off—paid and unpaid—on employee well-being and job performance."

Another good resource is *The 5 Languages of Appreciation in the Workplace: Empowering Organizations by Encouraging People* by Gary Chapman and Paul White. This book assists you in improving workplace relationships merely by learning your employees' language of appreciation.

CHAPTER FOUR

Accountability and Performance

"When your work speaks for itself, don't interrupt." — Henry J. Kaiser

One of the key measurements of accountability is employee performance. Everyone has a job description in the workplace, from the CEO to the janitor. If that job description isn't executed with the expectancy that when performed at the highest level of proficiency possible it will benefit the company's bottom line, then it is just another piece of paper. Job performance is defined by the Business Dictionary as:

"The work-related activities expected of an employee and how well those activities were executed. Many business personnel directors assess the job performance of each employee on an annual or quarterly basis in order to help them identify suggested areas for improvement."[20]

---

[20] http://www.businessdictionary.com/definition/job-performance.html

So, the productiveness of these work-related activities must be measured and employees have to be held responsible for their valuable contribution of *sweat equity*. Managing consequences of underperformance is also an invaluable tool to establish a culture of accountability. It allows management the opportunity to reacquaint an employee with their job description and the company's performance expectations. Also, management can retool an employee through training, education, motivation, mentoring, or counseling for on-the-job success.

Reform Support Network, in their article titled *Performance Management: Ensuring Accountability for Results*, defines performance management as "a systemic approach to ensure quality and progress toward organizational goals by aligning structures, processes, and routines through a set of reinforcing activities that enable an agency to methodically and routinely monitor the connection between the work underway and the outcomes sought."[21] In regards to accountability, they also state that "accountability for results" is "making decisions to continue, improve or end practices based on data; implementing incentives tied to performance; and engaging and communicating results with internal and external stakeholders."

Our premise in Chapter Four is that accountability and performance go hand-in-hand when examining your accountability culture to determine if your stakeholders are resourcefully contributing to the overall success of your business. This is a report card of sorts that determines the periodic wellbeing of your supervisory, operations, production, and administrative staff; resources; management initiatives and the processes that contribute to the company's overall performance.

In their article titled *Building Accountability and Transparency in Performance Management*, CRG

---

[21] https://www2.ed.gov/about/inits/ed/implementation-support-unit/tech-assist/performance-management-ensuring-accountability.pdf

emPerform writes, "It should be every business owner's goal to have an empowered and motivated team working for them. An energized team tends to be productive and provides excellent customer service, which is great for business. While there are plenty of different strategies in creating a dynamic workplace, two of the biggest factors are accountability and transparency." This implies that communication is key when fostering employee/management relationships that are built on truth. You must know the accurate numbers and use analytical tools such as evaluations, metrics, analysis, assessments, and employee feedback to properly ascertain the health of your business, so that you can build wealth in your business. Use these tools to empower and engage your employees instead of judging them or creating a culture of fear, anxiety and mystery.

Frank Ancharski in his article titled, *Managing Staff Performance and Accountability*, lists the following tools for your employee performance toolkit. *The Employee Performance Agreement* is a document where you can do a form of goal setting. This simple tool helps you chart a course of success throughout the year, not just at year end. The document may include a *Goals and Desires Statement, Specific Work Performance Expectations, Specific Behavior Performance Expectations, and an Agreement Statement.* (Frank suggests that the agreement may include promise language between the supervisor and employee to meet or exceed goals, for professional development and other essentials as deemed necessary.)

Frank also cited "trust" as another vital component. It is equally important because it empowers you to facilitate managing and engaging employees (your human capital). It is developed when you build a professional relationship with your staff. It is not something that is arbitrarily given but must be earned over the course of time. In our fast-paced workplace, this may seem impossible but investing in people is a priority especially when you are building trust. We will discuss this later on in this chapter.

The power of recognition

Employees are often recognized for their exemplary performance on the job by both their peers and management. In the past, recognition was often equated to monetary bonuses or elaborate awarding events. In our contemporary cost-conscious work environments, employee recognition can be delivered on a more reasonable scale. Immediate recognition, such as a hardy congratulations for a job well done or a heartfelt "thank you" for working overtime is often all that is needed to make an employee knowledgeable of your appreciation for their efforts. This is important because it keeps them happy and happy employees are more productive. Recognition of job mastery nurtures employee loyalty, promotes collaboration, and boosts morale.

Recognition in an environment where positive reinforcement and productive feedback is celebrated is a workplace where everyone wants to be! Here's a snapshot of Glassdoor's *2018 Best Places to Work: 11*[th]

Edition compiled from employee-submitted reviews and employee comments in support of their selection.

#1. Bain & Co. — "I am blown away by the culture of this company and tremendously proud to be a Bainie," says one employee of the Boston-headquartered consulting firm.

#2. Zoom Video Communications — "Great benefits, great work environment and free snacks," says one employee of the San Jose, California-based provider of video conferencing and group meeting IT services. "Absolutely blown away by Eric [Yuan] - the CEO," another employee writes. "Incredible leader, humble, has an open door policy, and is a true team player. The company culture has been built off those principles and even through the major growth stage the company is at right now, they have still been able to maintain that as the foundation."

#3. In-and-Out Burger — "You get to work with amazing people and you have great opportunities to advance both in store and corporate," says one employee of the California-headquartered fast-food company. "They offer great training and have a great support structure."

#4. Procore Technologies — "Procore has all of the typical, new age tech company perks: unlimited time off, snacks, beer, bring your dog to work and free lunch on Wednesdays," writes one reviewer of the cloud-based construction management software company based in Carpinteria, California. "The culture is pretty easy-going and everyone is pretty relaxed for the most part, depending on the department."

#5. Boston Consulting Group — "Best work and life balance, amazing benefits, amazing people and most importantly, a people-focused company," writes one employee of the Boston-based consulting group. "Excellent colleagues and work environment. Great place to develop your skills and grow as a professional," writes a second reviewer."

#6. LinkedIn — "The professional social media site has a culture that is really positive," one employee writes.

"People genuinely seem happy to be working there," the review continues. "Employees are talented, driven and very smart.'"

#7. Facebook — "Tons of incredible perks: benefits, time off, autonomy," one reviewer writes of the social media giant. "They are far ahead of the curve when it comes to diversity and inclusion. From the minute you start, you'll feel comfortable and valued. Management genuinely cares about your development and personal goals."

"The company says it surveys its employees twice a year to better understand what they want from the employer — and LinkedIn tweaks its practices and policies based on that feedback."

Great people, benefits, work environment, training, and approachable leadership were the key components to employee happiness at these stellar companies. If we put your company under a microscope, would it get an A$^+$ in all or any of these areas from your employees? This is a great place to start when building an accountability culture that recognizes the power of recognition.

It is also a major contributor to employee retention. Employee incentive programs that consist of the company offering raises, bonuses, and stock options for performance recognition is a great way to show your appreciation for an employee's loyalty and outstanding job performance.

Employee recognition can also provide motivation for employees to improve their production through self-improvement. Companies can incentivize learning by rewarding employees that go the extra mile to be better equipped for optimal job performance.

Here are a few ways that are all inclusive and timely incentives to recognize employees for their diligence in the workplace:

- Monetary bonuses

- Giving employees company branded giveaways

- Free lunch and snack days

- Having employee appreciation events and days

- Celebrating birthdays, work anniversaries, births, and special events

- Sending "thank you" emails and cards

- Having an Employee Recognition wall

Having fun on the job is not a passé or outdated tactic when attempting to positively influence employee performance. Recognition is a powerful tool that employers often disregard because they are too focused on the outcome instead of the personnel who can improve the results of that outcome. When you invest in people, you are making a wise investment.

Communication: why is it important?

In today's workplace, communication is crucial when attempting to maximize employee performance. Is your work environment one that promotes open dialog or supports constructive guidance or counseling? The sender, message context, receiver, content and delivery all play an important part in the workplace communication cycle. One thing that is often overlooked in this cycle is the environment where the communication is taking place. If it's a toxic environment where employees are afraid of being openly reprimanded for their mistakes and micromanagement is the preferred style of the command center then open and honest communication may be stifled or nonexistent.

If you want to build a healthy workplace where accountability and communication flourishes, here are a few things to consider:

- Get to know your employees' personalities and understand their communication styles.

- Create a receptive environment.

- Be cognizant of your favorite means for communication.

- Encourage feedback to measure the effectiveness of your preferred style of communication.

- Offer comprehensive training when you are introducing a new process, product or service, software, or resource.

- Have a plan to resolve conflict quickly and make employees aware of that process or procedure before you have to use it.

- Hold employees accountable for identifying problems and also providing workable solutions as suggestions.

- When delivering constructive criticism, make sure that it is done privately and in a nonthreatening manner. Use this opportunity to empower the employee to make the necessary adjustment in a supportive atmosphere.

- Be a good listener. Be slow to provide feedback and allow the employee to share how they feel without repercussions or fear of retaliation.

- Work collaboratively to develop new employee policies and procedures.

- Be appreciative and don't be afraid to show it.

Poor communication in the workplace throws a monkey wrench onto your organizational effectiveness and efficiency. Staff member become lethargic and unmotivated which sets the atmosphere for the "blame game" to take precedence over what everyone should be focusing on—production and performance.

If you want the opposite effect in your workplace environment, you should concentrate on building effective teams where effective communication is a priority. Managers who are "master communicators" are better at managing their teams. In this kind of environment, respect and trust are built when everyone knows that their opinion is important and that they are being listened to, regardless of where they fall on the organizational chart. This allows the employee to feel that valued and when that kicks in, innovation is a welcomed byproduct. When employees are innovative, the company experiences growth, both internally and externally. Also, all the stakeholders benefit from new ideas, new product or service developments, and streamlined budgets.

Communication is important for a host of reasons but most importantly, it is important because the overall success of your company depends on it to thrive.

Building trust

Trust in the workplace should be defined by both the employer and employee. A leader has the responsibility to cultivate an environment where trust can take root and grow based on their willingness to model the appropriate behavior. Your employees should know that they will be treated fairly and respected.

A leader is trustworthy when they do what they say they are going to do; are friendly and approachable; work hard to show respect for their employees and their ideas; show unwavering support for their employees; are quick to remediate when mistakes are made; and make sure that their words and actions agree all of the time. In exchange, an employee should respect a leader who motivates and empowers them to perform at their highest capability. Be committed to the company's primary goals and objectives and strive to make the company a successful one.

The 2019 Edelman Trust Barometer Global Report is an annual global trust survey which measures the prevailing attitudes about the state of trust in business, government, NGOs and the media. The Trust Barometer surveys over 33,000 respondents from 28 different countries. According to Edelman intelligence, "The 2019 Edelman Trust Barometer reveals that trust has changed profoundly in the past year with "my employer" emerging as the most trusted institution. Globally, "my employer" (75 percent) is significantly more trusted than NGOs (57 percent), business (56 percent), government (48 percent) and media (47 percent).

"The last decade has seen a loss of faith in traditional authority figures and institutions," said Richard Edelman, president and CEO of Edelman. "More recently, people have lost confidence in the social platforms that fostered peer-to-peer trust. These forces have led people to shift their trust to the relationships within their control, most notably their employers." Wow! It appears as though the world has more faith in CEOs bringing about change in their respective communities, both economically and socially while increasing profits at the same time than the government. Edelman goes on to say, "This is the emergence of the new contract between employee and employer, which we call Trust at Work," said Edelman. "This contract is predicated on companies taking four specific actions: lead on change, establish an audacious goal that attracts socially-minded employees and make it a core business objective; empower and keep employees directly informed on the issues of the day and give them a voice on your channels; start locally and make a positive impact in the communities in which you operate; and CEO leadership which involves speaking up directly on issues of the day. Smart companies will heed the call to build trust from the inside out with employees as the focal point."

As we closely examine the top seven companies listed in *Glassdoor's 2018 Best Places to Work: 11ᵗʰ Edition,* it's obvious that's where we are headed. But we are not there yet! Inc. had an interesting article written by Marissa Levin, Founder and CEO, Successful Culture, titled *Nine Leadership Behaviors That Lose Employee Trust and Respect.* Levin identified the "most polarizing, destructive behaviors leaders can exhibit" and they are as follows:

> 1. **Inauthenticity.** Authentic leaders stay true to what they believe. According to Harvard Business School professor and authentic leadership expert Bill George, authentic

leaders remain true to their values and mission even in the face of difficulty.

2. **False promises.** Leaders must be careful about the carrots they dangle to motivate their employees. If a leader makes a promise, his or her employees have every right to expect follow-through.

3. **Ambiguity.** Employees require specificity when it comes to communicating direction. Ambiguity signals two things: lack of clarity regarding direction and secrecy. Both of these impressions drive mistrust and skepticism. The clearer you can be regarding your vision and direction, the quicker you will engage others.

4. **One-way communication.** In traditional, hierarchical organizations, information flowed from the top down, through a tightly controlled funnel. Employees simply did their jobs and received the precise information that leadership wanted

them to have. Today, employees have a powerful voice. In healthy cultures, they are empowered to contribute ideas and observations. Employees have valuable feedback and want to be heard.

5. **Personal agendas or ego-driven leadership.** Leaders require thick skins to power through setbacks and negativity. They also require strong self-confidence because of the non-believers who question their abilities and would find pleasure in seeing them fail. However, leaders have to check their egos at the door and ensure they subjugate their own personal agendas for the greater good of the organization.

6. **Anger.** There is no place in leadership for uncontrolled anger. It conveys fear, disrespect, lack of control and lack of concern for those who are on the receiving end.

7. **Refusing to delegate or empower.** Leadership is a team effort. When employees join your organization to support your vision, they bring experience and skills that can move your strategy forward. It can be difficult to release control, knowing that others may not do things exactly as you would. However, one person—or even a team of leaders in a growing organization—can't complete all tasks. Effective delegation enables you to stay focused on what you do best or what you love the most.

8. **An attitude of superiority or lack of appreciation.** Employees see their bosses and the C-level community very differently from the way they see themselves. In companies, there is a line of demarcation between leadership and the rest of the company, even if they leaders don't intend to create such a division. As our organizations grow, it's easy for us to get

disconnected from our employees. We have to be intentional about creating appreciation strategies.

9. **Playing favorites.** One of the most demoralizing leadership behaviors is favoritism. While every organization has "linchpins" who are essential in holding the company together, ideally organizations should aim to be "process-centric" rather than "hero-centric." When companies revolve around a handful of heroes, the remaining employees can begin to feel that they are disposable.[22]

We recommend that you focus on doing the opposite of each one of these destructive behaviors in order to build trust in your company. Your employees will appreciate your efforts and hopefully, you will get premium performance for your efforts.

---

[22] https://www.inc.com/marissa-levin/9-leadership-behaviors-that-lose-employee-trust-and-respect.html

Accountability Matters Case Study Three: Lack of Communication and Transparency

How Does a Lack of Communication Influence Employee Turnover?

The lack of communication in the workplace is a major contributor to the disintegration of the employer/employee relationship and creates an atmosphere of distrust. Managers' lack of communication and transparency contributes to CSRs leaving the call center.

In this case study, we will take a look at the dissertation, *Employee Retention in an Organization Call Center*, to get a snapshot of the contributing factor to high turnover rates in this industry based on a lack of communication and transparency. This subtheme refers to the perception that managers' lack of communication and transparency contributes to call center CSRs leaving the call center. Lack of communication and transparency was mentioned five times in four interviews.

Feedback — There is a lack of communication and transparency in the call center work environment.

Reference: Research Question One— "What working conditions contribute to call center CSRs leaving the call center?"

Participant 12 said:

"I think inclusion is very important. This is a small company; its main focus right now is to grow. It seems like everything, every decision, everything that's done to make the company grow is done in the shadows. The majority of the employees hear about it after the fact, and that break between the people who are making the decisions and the people who it affects...that's a major player in the turnover. If we sign new groups and all of a sudden, we have to do new things, no one tells the people about the new things until someone calls into the call center and they realize I have no idea what this person is talking about."

Participant 15 explained:

"[There is] no communication whatsoever. It's one-sided. Even if we do communicate it's a wall and we are talking to that wall. There's someone there, but that person is just not listening. And I spoke with my manager about this. He called me in for a meeting and wanted to know what we can do. I told him I don't think I want to waste time in this meeting. I have cases to do. I know that from previous experience, I've had meetings like this, and nothing has been done. So, if you know this is just going to be a time where I talk, you write it down, and you say, okay you've done a little work today… I told him that and he was staring at me. I had to be truthful. I told him to let me know so I could go match my cases because there were many times, I said I've had this conversation in the past, and nothing has been done. So, I don't want a conversation to paper meeting, I want a conversation to conversation meeting, an action meeting."

Feedforward

A lack of communication and transparency can be remedied, but it takes an intentional effort to do so from the top to the bottom. This effort must be based on a reestablished trust between all the stakeholders. Due to the frequent turnover in the call centers, employees expect to not be heard. Often their contributions are devalued because it has become the expectation of management that they won't be around long enough because of the nature of their jobs. Rewrite your business story by revamping your employee retention and reward programs with the intention of investing in all employees to build a culture that fosters employee growth and performance.

Follow-up

Interested in improving your employee engagement? Take a peek at the following videos by Bob Kelleher, an award-winning author, speaker, thought leader, and consultant. Bob travels around the globe sharing his insights on employee engagement, leadership, and workforce trends. He is also the President and Founder of The Employee Engagement Group.

Employee Engagement – Who's Sinking Your Boat? (https://www.youtube.com/watch?v=y4nwoZ02AJM)

Employee Engagement: Why Is Your Boat Still Sinking (November 10, 2016)

https://www.youtube.com/watch?v=FvDKh31k1fM

Here's a quote from Bob Kelleher on employee engagement.

"Engagement is an outcome of a mutual commitment between an organization and an employee where the organization is helping the employee reach his/her potential, while the individual is helping the organization also be successful. This mutual commitment is what leads to 'discretionary effort' which is the magic dust that really drives business performance."

CHAPTER FIVE

Accountability and Culture

"A culture of accountability makes a good organization great and a great organization unstoppable." — Henry Evan

Culture is the personality and behavior of an organization. It's what makes a business exclusive and is a portrait of its ethics, traditions, principles, communications, actions, and attitudes. It is reflected in its internal and external communications, from the water cooler to the company's community outreach. It is everyone's responsibility and the true test of accountability is reflected in the organization's profit and loss statement.

Investopedia states that "corporate culture refers to the beliefs and behaviors that determine how a company's employees and management interact and handle outside business transactions. Often, corporate culture is implied, not expressly defined, and develops organically over time from the cumulative traits of the people the company hires. A company's culture will be reflected in its dress code, business hours, office setup, employee benefits, turnover, hiring decisions, treatment of clients, client satisfaction, and every other aspect of operations."

Over the last few chapters, we have discussed what good accountability looks like and what contributes to developing an effective culture in your organization. Building an accountability culture is a deliberate action requiring the collaboration of all of the organization's stakeholders. In other words, teamwork is what makes or breaks a company's ability to be accountable. People are a nonexpendable asset and the way they think and act determines your results.

Partnerships in Leadership in the article, *A Culture of Accountability,* states the following:

"The best kind of culture is a Culture of Accountability where people demonstrate high levels of ownership to think and act in the manner necessary to achieve organizational results. The defining characteristic of this kind of culture is that *people voluntarily assume their own accountability*. Rather than having accountability forced upon them, they enthusiastically take it upon themselves. That's right, they are neither commanded to be accountable nor kept under surveillance until "called to account" for their actions. In a Culture of Accountability, people at every level of the organization are personally committed to achieving key results targeted by the team or organization, and they never wait to be asked for a progress report or a follow-up plan. Instead, they report proactively and follow-up constantly, diligently measuring their own progress because they have internalized their commitment to achieving results. Their mantra— *"What else can I do to achieve the desired results?"*—leads them to continually find answers, develop solutions, overcome obstacles, and triumph over any trouble that might come along. And, as you would expect, everyone holds everyone accountable for results."[23]

---

[23] https://www.partnersinleadership.com/insights-publications/a-culture-of-accountability/

It is implied in the previous statement that people who are energized, informed, empowered and valued will be more motivated to assume responsibility for their actions and the byproduct is an innovative community of problem solvers and intrapreneurs.

If you aren't there yet, you can get there if you are willing to do the work and change the culture. According to *Change the Culture, Change the Game* by Roger Connors and Tom Smith, "To change your results, you have to change your culture—that is, you have to change the experiences, beliefs, and actions of your people."

Does culture start at the top or with you?

Accountability is a bilateral responsibility and building a sustainable accountability culture is the responsibility of everyone. The origin of this responsibility for building culture depends on the organizational structure of your company. In a vertical organization, the business has a traditional top-down structure, with an owner or CEO at the top, mid-level management, and supervisors, with regular employees at the bottom of the pyramid. In a horizontal organization, the business structure is flat. In this structure, there are few managers and the employees have more authority.

Collaboration and team building are more conducive in a horizontal organization because employees have been empowered to make decisions and manage their outcomes. Building accountability can occur organically. In a vertical organization, collaboration and team building occur when it is a management directive. The difference is in the effort it will take from the top down to make the change and how the transformation initiatives are implemented uninformedly in each department.

How to build a culture of accountability

In the article titled *Creating a Culture of Accountability,* Lever stated, "Creating accountability in the workplace means creating a culture where everyone is assuming responsibility at work. Achieving this result depends heavily on good communication; if your team is on the same page then a sense of unity will make everyone more comfortable on the job. Truly, accountability is the key to driving a high-performance culture. When expectations are fair and obvious and employees know how to show accountability at work, they will want to do their best!"[24]

Building a culture of accountability requires teamwork, no matter how authority flows within the organization. Effective leadership is the key to its success and effective leaders cultivating accountable employees. They do this through mentorship, being inquisitive, seeking feedback, being communicative, encouraging peer coaching, setting clear precise goals that are obtainable and providing timely feedback.

Accountable leaders are honest and transparent. They are quick to assume responsibility for their actions, both right and wrong. They do not over or under

---

[24] https://www.lever.co/blog/creating-a-culture-of-accountability/

commit, avoid responsibility and they do not procrastinate.

According to Cathy McCullough in *Quick Tips for Building Accountability*, leaders should take into account the following accountability tips:

- Realize that building accountability is not about punishment. You'll have to make sure leaders understand this key point.

- Define, with great clarity, who's doing what. Roles and responsibilities should be clearly identified (the Job Scorecard is a great way to do this). When things overlap, give a further definition as to who's doing what and who reports to whom, what the expectations are for each party, etc.

- When you set your strategic priorities, each one has only one person "driving" it. Not two, not three. One. Others will certainly help by perhaps having some individual priorities to accomplish, but only one person is ultimately accountable for driving the initiative forward.

- Watch for confusion relative to competing priorities and sort these out as needed.

- Create a culture where the expectation to openly share and communicate is the norm and not the exception.

- Design pathways to help people interact toward the achievement of higher results.

- Always help people identify individual priorities they should be working on.

- Simply do not accept victim mentality—at all. Victim mentality feeds the lack of accountability.

- Do not accept finger-pointing. Instead, create a culture where you can actually talk wisely and positively about failures.

- Be a visible leader. Connect with people. You can't build team accountability if people don't really know you. Transparency and accountability are both critical in high-performance cultures.

- The state of being accountable is a mindset. As a leader, you should start with yourself. Always accept responsibility for your actions, even if it makes you feel vulnerable. Your team will thank you for it and follow your lead.

- If you want your employees held to account, you need to be accountable to your team first.

- Set goals that are realistic. If you set goals that are stretch goals or hard to obtain, it could lead to people "fudging" their results as they don't want to let the team down.

- Reinforce that the culture is to ensure the team is reaching your goals. Keep the focus on achieving your goals rather than the consequences of not achieving them, to keep positive momentum.[25]

Simple steps for building accountability

One of the common keys to building an accountability culture is establishing a sense of comrade amongst employees through team building. Some of the benefits of building a team are it improves communication, encourages creativity, develops problem-solving skills, motivates employees, increases productivity and increases collaboration. These are all building blocks for an effective accountability culture.

In an article on Inc., Partnership in Leadership defined *The Five C's for Building Team Accountability* as:

- COMMON PURPOSE—Discuss the importance—connect to WHY— "Why does this matter?"

---

[25] https://www.rhythmsystems.com/blog/quick-tips-for-building-accountability

- CLEAR EXPECTATIONS—Clarity expectations together—Get clear about WHO and WHAT— "What does success look like?"

- COMMUNICATION and ALIGNMENT— Focus and align everyone involved— Communicate HOW— "How are we going to achieve success?"

- COLLABORATION—Collaborate and adjust as needed—Monitor progress and COACH— "Are we on track and what adjustments are needed?"

- CONSEQUENCES—Make results and consequences visible—Assess the RESULTS— "How did we do and what did we learn?"

These suggestions set the foundation for building or changing the culture of accountability with team building as its foundation.

Let's take a moment to review why having accountability is important. It accelerates employee performance. Accountability helps you measure the success of your company. It gives employees value, confidence, and promotes their intellectual growth. It helps upper and middle-level managers and employees to be responsible. It provides an incubator for innovation and problem-solving and most importantly, it gives them the satisfaction of accomplishing the company's goals. What's more, it increases productivity and that's always good for business.

Accountability Matters Case Study Four: Poor Leadership Styles Create Tension

How Do Problems With Management Influence Employee Turnover?

The lack of communication in the workplace is a major contributor to disintegration of the employer/employee relationship and creates an atmosphere of distrust. Managers' lack of communication and transparency contributes to call center CSRs leaving the call center.

In this case study, we will take a look at the dissertation, *Employee Retention in an Organization Call Center*, to get a snapshot of the contributing factor to high turnover rates in this industry based on a lack of communication and transparency. This subtheme refers to the perception that poor leadership styles create tension which contributes to call center CSRs leaving their job. This subtheme was mentioned nine times in seven interviews.

Feedback — *Poor leadership styles create tension.*

Reference: Research Question One — "What working conditions contribute to call center CSRs leaving the call center?"

Participant 18 said, "It definitely creates a lot of tension because you're looking at your management team like, 'I have so much that I'm doing, and you're not really helping. You're telling me to reach out to you but when I do, you're not really giving any great advice or anything that I should do.' It's more like a, 'Let me know so that I can look at you work.' Or something like that."

Participant 10 stated that, "The previous supervisor in the call center was very authoritarian. This really did not go well with a lot of the people in the department because the supervisor before them was very laid back. It was a complete change in management. I think you just have to try to have management that's consistent."

Feedforward

Consistency is the key when establishing a professional relationship of trust with your employees. When upper-level management makes establishing trust a priority, it will start a cultural paradigm shift in the company for accountability.

Follow-up

The American Psychological Association is a great resource for coping with stress and tension on the job. Check out _Coping With Stress at Work_ as well as _Work-Life Fit Linked to Employee Engagement, Motivation and Job Satisfaction_.

CHAPTER SIX

Final Thoughts and Recommendations

Chapter Six Accountability Does Matter in the Workplace

"Good men are bound by conscience and liberated by accountability." — Wes Fessler

Final Thoughts

In the beginning of our journey, my mission was to give you enough evidence to answer the question "Why does accountability matter in the workplace?" Let's take a stroll down memory lane and look at a snapshot of what we've covered in Chapters One through Five.

In Chapter One, we addressed the meaning of accountability and how it is designed to improve the workplace environment. We also looked at the difference between accountability and responsibility and why organizational leadership should expect it to be an integral part of their community.

In Chapter Two, we addressed accountability from an employee's perspective and how an employee's interaction with management, human resources and their peers set the pace for an accountability culture that works in your particular industry. We also discussed the importance of the degree of accountability managers should assume versus an employee. In each scenario, accountability starts with the individual. We also listed several ways accountability can be increased in the workplace.

In Chapter Three, we focused on how motivation influences accountability in the workplace. We defined what employee motivation should look like and set the parameters for how accountability and motivation should work together in a linear work environment. We discussed various effective methods that have worked for a host of companies, whether they are a start-up or established business. Productivity and motivation and how they relate to each other to improve the level of employee buy-in to a company's goals and objectives were also examined in this chapter.

In Chapter Four, we discussed how accountability impacts employee performance. First, we defined what performance is and how to overtly recognize good and great performance in a culture that fosters employee accountability. The importance of communication was discussed and how it contributes to a stress-free work environment. Finally, we discussed the importance of building the kind of trust between employers and employees that promote innovative and intrapreneurial ideas and results.

In Chapter Five, the word "culture" was defined and its origination deliberated. The various building blocks for a healthy and productive accountability culture were discussed. For those companies who are re-focusing, re-strategizing, and re-energizing, we have laid a solid roadmap for you to start the building process. Throughout this powerful resource, we have also spent quite a bit of time clarifying the role of management in creating, implementing, and maintaining an accountability culture.

Behind each of these chapters, we have shared an Accountability Matters Case Study focusing on my dissertation: *Employee Retention in an Organization Call Center.* Each case study shares employee observations *(Feedback)* about an accountability problem identified in their workplace. We provided a brief discussion *(Feedforward)* of the problem with a viable solution based on our research on accountability. In conclusion, we made a recommendation *(Follow-up)* of a resource that could assist you in handling that problem if it should occur in your work environment.

In this chapter, we will conclude *Accountability in the Workplace: Why Does it Matter?* with a case study on the popular television show, *Undercover Boss.*

It was my desire that you would leave this literary experience with a better understanding of the importance of accountability in the modern workplace; the modern worker's best posture in an accountability driven workplace; the benefits of employee motivation and accountability and how it affects employee productivity and performance; how to build an accountability culture and last but not least, examining management's responsibility for accountability in the workplace.

It was very important that I adequately communicate the idea that accountability in the workplace is an asset for both the employer and employee. In the 21st century, it is a vital position for your company to assume for growth. The lifeblood of a company is the people who co-labor with you to meet your fiscal objectives. When you recognize them for the value they bring to the table, they recognize the possibility of their career dreams coming true right there in the petri dish of your accountability culture. They work harder, longer, and better because they have a vested interest in helping you achieve your goals. It's important to consistently communicate to them their worth to your organization. It's the fuel that keeps their engine running at its highest level of efficiency because a paycheck isn't always enough.

In the words of Jim Rohn, entrepreneur, author and motivational speaker, "Communication is two or more people working together to find the common ground understanding. And when they find that common ground, they are positioned to have tremendous power together." Remember to position yourself for "tremendous power" through fostering an accountability culture that works for everyone. It has been my experience that you will be glad that you did!

Accountability Matters
Case Study Five:
Undercover Boss

What Would You Uncover If You Became an Undercover Boss?

The first episode of *Undercover Boss* was aired on CBS on February 7, 2010. Executive producer Eli Holzman wanted America and company management executives to see what really goes on behind the scenes in some of the major corporations and businesses in the nation. In this television program, high level corporate executives disguise themselves as new employees or interns to find out what their employees really think about them and the company. This two-time Emmy Award-winning series has been eye-opening for them, their company employees, and their viewers.

In this case study, we will take a look at the show's premise and how effective it has been at accomplishing its mission.

Feedback

We chose an article on <u>Looper</u> titled, *The Untold Truth of Undercover Boss*[26] as our resource for feedback.

---

[26]   https://www.looper.com/14490/untold-truth-undercover-boss/?utm_campaign=clip

Feedback — "Skeptics believe many aspects of the show are fake or exaggerated, but producers and most show participants insist otherwise. We've uncovered the truth."

Looper had this to say about the show:

- *Undercover Boss* uses the genius tactic of pretending to be some sort of "win your own franchise" game show—complete with a fake host in some episodes—to dissuade employees from figuring out they're on the show. Amazingly, few workers see through this flimsy facade. Maybe it's because in every episode, the bosses must change their appearances.

- One of the biggest questions people ask is whether the work scenarios the bosses have to engage in are completely staged. The answer is yes and no. According to Holzman, the show obviously tries to pick job scenarios with good

TV optics, but the bosses don't know "exactly where they're going to go, and they don't know exactly with whom they're going to work, because we want them to [have] an authentic experience."

- Some companies have actually implemented positive steps to drive change, such as providing a financial incentive for employees to improve. Checkers CEO Rick Silva started "giving bonuses directly to team members, not just the branch managers." Dan DiZio, CEO of Philly Pretzel Factory, discovered a brand new, hot-selling product after uncovering a "rogue franchisee" that was marketing and selling an unsanctioned pepperoni pretzel roll. DiZio wasn't pleased with the free-wheeling franchisee, but he also took its transgression as a sign that he'd become an "out of touch" boss.

- The most beloved part of every *Undercover Boss* episode is the ending. The head honcho reveals his true identity and starts making it rain with cash, vacations, and college tuition payments for the employees who were duped by the elaborate ruse. It's a tearjerker every time, even if it is a cheap emotional trick.

Feedforward

Anytime a CEO or corporate executive takes time out of their busy schedule to go on a *seek and find* mission in disguise, assuming a fake identity, so that they can make their company better in front of millions of viewers is the highest level of accountability possible.

If you really want to know what's going on in your company communication is key. Your frontline employees are excellent resources when they can trust that they can share the truth about their personal and professional observations about the workplace. *Undercover Boss* is a good example of how when management assumes a position of accountability, everyone from the janitor to the chairman of the board win!

Follow-up

For more information on *Undercover Boss*, click here and here.

Undercover Boss has inspired corporate executives to go as far as to help save lives. In the case of Stephen Cloobeck, the founder and chairman of Diamond Resorts loved his experience so much that he did it twice. Cloobeck stated, "Being on *Undercover Boss* changed my life forever. I learned it's important to take care of as many people as possible."

As a result, he has contributed $2 million to his workers, $1 million of which came from his own pocket. He's paid for a worker's life-saving cancer treatments, and he has also started a special crisis fund for all his 5,600 employees. We hope that *Accountability in the Workplace: Why Does it Matter?* inspires you to follow in Cloobeck's footsteps. When people matter to you, your company's success matters to them!

About the Author

Angelica Pigman, DBA. is the founder and CEO of Classic AP Consultant. Dr. Angelica's mission is to teach others how to grow through faith and marketplace skills to enhance themselves and their business.

Dr. Pigman's journey began as a Provider Relations Advocate in the health care industry. She has logged nearly twenty years of experience in various areas of managed care (provider relations, retention account manager, quality improvement specialist, telephonic service coordinator and authorization coordinator).

In additional to her extensive experience, Dr. Angelica also has outstanding academic background that includes a Doctorate in Business Administration (Strategy & Innovation) from Capella University in Minnesota and a Masters in Business Management from Letourneau University in Houston. Dr. Angelica is also a Certified Life Coach from The Bloom Life Coach Institute.

Dr. Angelica's combination of academic qualifications, health care and coaching experience provides a strong foundation for the kind of work approach to business owners and helping others heal and thrive. The training she received from the Bloom Institute gave her a deep understanding of how we get stuck in negative patterns and settle for unfulfilled lives of mediocrity because we're disconnected from the full expression of our talents.

Additional Resources

Books

Supportive Accountability: How to Inspire People and Improve Performance by Sylvia Melena

CARE to Lead: How to Master and Implement Four Keys to Leadership: Communication, Accountability, Relationships and Example of Excellence by Alec McGalliard

The 4 Disciplines of Execution by Chris McChesney and Sean Covey

QBQ! The Question Behind the Question: Practicing Personal Accountability at Work and in Life by John G. Miller

Accountability: Taking Ownership of Your Responsibility by Henry Browning

The 5 Second Rule: Transform Your Life, Work, and Confidence with Everyday Courage by Mel Robbins

Change the Culture, Change the Game: The Breakthrough Strategy for Energizing Your Organization and Creating Accountability by Tom Smith and Roger Connors

Accountability, the Key to Driving a High-Performance Culture by Greg Bustin

The Oz Principle by Roger Connors

Accountability Leadership: How Great Leaders Build a High Performance Culture of Accountability and Responsibility by Di Worrall

Winning With Accountability: The Secret Language of High-Performing Organizations by Henry James Evans

Articles

Why Accountability Matters at Work by Sean Pomeroy

References

Backer, L. C. (2004). *Surveillance and control: Privatizing and Nationalizing Corporate Monitoring After Sarbanes-Oxley.* Mich. St. L. Rev., 327.

Birchall, C. (2011). *Introduction to 'Secrecy and Transparency': The Politics of Opacity and Openness.* Theory, Culture & Society, 28(7-8), 7-25.

Branco, M. C., & Delgado, C. (2012). *Business, Social Responsibility, and Corruption.* Journal of Public Affairs, 12(4), 357-365.

Coghlan, D., & Brannick, T. (2014). *Doing Action Research in Your Own Organization.* Sage.

De Sousa, L., Hindess, B., & Larmour, P. (Eds.). (2012). *Governments, NGOs and Anti-Corruption: The New Integrity Warriors.* Routledge.

Dowden, C. (2012). *Increasing Employee Accountability: The critical Role of Leadership.* The Human Resources Professional Association Ottawa Chapter Magazine. 10(4), 1.

Fink-Samnick, E. (2008). *Developing a Resilience Accountability Continuum: Part 2: Workplace.* Professional Case Management, 13(6), 338-343.

Gasper, D. (2016). *Ethics of Development.*

Grant, R. W., & Keohane, R. O. (2005). *Accountability and Abuses of Power in World Politics.* American Political Science Review, 99(1), 29-43.

Grimshaw, J, Baron, G, Mike, B & Edwards, N. (2006). *How to Combat a Culture of Excuses and Promote Accountability.* Strategy & Leadership, 34(5), p.11-18.

Hall, A. T., Frink, D. D., Ferris, G. R., Hochwarter, W. A., Kacmar, C. J., & Bowen, M. G. (2003).

Accountability in Human Resources Management. New Directions in Human Resource Management, 29-63.

Hood, C. (2010). *Accountability and Transparency: Siamese Twins, Matching Parts, Awkward Couple?* West European Politics, 33(5), 989-1009.

Hoskisson, R. E., Eden, L., Lau, C. M., & Wright, M. (2000). *Strategy in Emerging Economies.* Academy of Management Journal, 43(3), 249-267.

Koskinen, I. (2000). *Plans, Evaluation, and Accountability at the Workplace.* Sociological Research Online, 4(4), 1-17.

Leshner, A. I. (2009). *Accountability and Transparency.* Science, 324(5925), 313-313.

Mehri, C., Giampetro-Meyer, A., & Runnels, M. B. (2003). *One Nation, Indivisible: The Use of Diversity Report Cards to Promote Transparency, Accountability, and Workplace Fairness.* Fordham J. Corp. & Fin. L., 9, 395.

Mulgan, R. (2000). *'Accountability': An Ever-Expanding Concept?* Public Administration, 78(3), 555-573.

Mulgan, R. (2003). *Holding Power to Account: Accountability in Modern Democracies.* Springer.

Partners in Leadership. (2009). *Creating a Culture of Accountability.* Accessed from https://www.fmi.org/docs/fc_presentations/building_an_accountable_culture_white_paper.pdf?sfvrsn=2

Perry, J. L., & Christensen, R. K. (2015). *Handbook of Public Administration.* John Wiley & Sons.

Rubenstein, J. (2007). *Accountability in an Unequal World.* The Journal of Politics, 69(3), 616-632.

Simons, R. (2005). *Levers of Organization Design: How Managers Use Accountability Systems For Greater Performance and Commitment.* Harvard Business Press.

Solomon, J. (2007). *Corporate Governance and Accountability.* John Wiley & Sons.

Solove, D. J., Rotenberg, M., & Schwartz, P. M. (2006). *Privacy, Information, and Technology*. Aspen Publishers Online.

Tapscott, D., & Ticoll, D. (2003). *The Naked Corporation: How the Age of Transparency Will Revolutionize Business*. Simon and Schuster.

Townley, B., Cooper, D. J., & Oakes, L. (2003). *Performance Measures and the Rationalization of Organizations*. Organization studies, 24(7), 1045-1071.

Zhang, I. X. (2007). *Economic Consequences of the Sarbanes–Oxley Act of 2002*. Journal of Accounting and Economics, 44(1), 74-115.

www.ingramcontent.com/pod-product-compliance
Lightning Source LLC
Chambersburg PA
CBHW061732050726
47598CB00002B/447